The PMP Notebook

A Study Companion Based on the 6th edition PMBOK® Guide

By Kaye I. Smith-Bedeau, PMP

The PMP Notebook

By Kaye I. Smith-Bedeau, PMP

Published by Triple Constraint Publications.

ISBN-13: 978-0-9998611-0-3

This book may be purchased for educational, business, or sales promotional use. For more information, contact us at Kayesmithpmp@gmail.com

Dedication

To my parents Paulet and Winston Smith who is always there when I need them and the best support system anyone can have. To my very first best friend, Smitty, who also happens to be my big brother. Andre, my wonderful husband.

Everyone who is taking the exam, good luck.

TABLE OF CONTENTS

Exam Framework

The exam consists of five areas which also relate the five-project management process:

1. Initiating the project-13%
2. Planning the Project- 24%
3. Executing the Project- 30%
4. Monitoring and Controlling the Project- 25%
5. Closing the Project- 8%

Looking at the percentage, you should focus studying on the Executing and Monitoring and Controlling of the project since that has the highest percentile.

There is a total of 175 scored questions and 25 un-scored (pretest) question. The pretest questions are basically questions that they want to test out for future exams.

THE FUNDAMENTALS OF PROJECT MANAGEMENT

WHAT ARE CHARACTERISTICS OF A PROJECT?

- Projects are temporary. Meaning that every project has a definite beginning and a definite end
- Projects are usually a unique product or service- something that has not been done before and has a unique result
- Performed by people
- Progressive Elaboration- because projects are unique, they are continuously and constantly modified, improved and details are added as more information is known about the project. This is also called rolling wave planning
- Planned, executed and controlled
- Projects drive change in organizations to achieve strategic goals
- Projects enable business value creation

WHY INITIATE PROJECTS?

- To solve problems
- To take an advantage of an opportunity

WHAT IS PROJECT MANAGEMENT?

- The application of knowledge, skills, tools, and techniques to project activities to meet project requirements
- To accomplish the activities, five process groups used: initiating, planning, executing, monitoring and control and closing
- Managing projects include:
    - Identifying requirements
    - Addressing needs, concerns, and expectations of stakeholders in a project
    - Maintaining communications among stakeholders. This includes setting up and carrying out the communication
    - Managing stakeholder expectations of the project deliverables
    - Balancing project constraints such as scope, quality, schedule, budget, resources, and risks

Importance of Project Management

- Meet business objectives
- Satisfy stakeholder expectations
- Be more predictable
- Increase chances of success
- Deliver the right products at the right time
- Resolve problems and issues
- Respond to risks in a timely manner
- Optimize the use of organizational resources
- Identify, recover or terminate failing projects
- Manage constraints
- Balance the influence of constraints on the project
- Manage change in better manner

Program Management

- A group of related projects and/or subprograms that are managed in a way to gain benefits and control instead of managing them individually
- Program management concentrates on determining the way multiple projects should be managed

Portfolio Management

- A collection of projects, program, sub-portfolios, and operations that are grouped together for effective management of the work to meet strategic business objectives

Project Management Office (PMO)

- A dedicated department that centralizes the management of projects
- Standardizes policies, methodologies, and templates for projects within the organization
- Provides guidance to others and support on how to manage projects. Also, trains individuals in managing projects within the organization.

- Responsible for managing projects within the organization and provides project managers to facilitate the project

Organizational Project management (OPM) and Strategies

- Portfolio management aligns portfolios with organizational strategies by selecting the right programs or projects, prioritizing the work, and providing the needed resources
- Program management harmonizes its program components and controls interdependencies in order to realize specified benefits
- Project management enables the achievement of organizational goals and objectives

Operations Management

- Operations management focuses on the management of ongoing production or goods and/or services

Organizational Project management

- Portfolio management aligns portfolios with organizational strategies by selecting the right programs or projects, prioritizing the work, and providing the need resources
- Program management harmonizes its program components and controls interdependencies in order to realize specified benefits
- Project management enables the achievement of organizational goals and objectives

The Role of a Project Manager

- A project manager is someone is assigned by the organization to lead a team that is responsible the delivering project objections and deliverables
- The project manager responsibility is to satisfy the task, team and individual needs. They are the link between strategy and the team
- Project managers must the three major competencies
    - Technical project management- the knowledge, skills, and behaviors related to specific domains of project, program and portfolio management
    - Leadership- The knowledge, skills, and behaviors needed to guide, motivate, and direct a team, to help an organization achieve its business goals
    - Strategic and business management- The knowledge of and expertise in the industry and organization that enhanced performance and better delivers business outcomes.
- Interpersonal skills project managers must possess, but not limited to are:

- Team building
- Motivation
- Communication
- Influencing
- Decision making
- Political and cultural awareness
- Negotiation
- Trust building
- Conflict management
- Coaching

Project and development Life Cycles

- Defined as the beginning and the end of a project, or from its initiation to its closure
- Defines what work should be done in each phase
- What should be involved in each phase
- Also referred to the performing organization's or department's methodology for projects
- Depending on the industry, there can many different types of project life cycles
- Project life cycles can be predictive or adaptive. Within a project life cycle, there are generally one or more phases of the development of the project, service or result which is called development life cycle
- Development life cycles can be predictive, incremental, adaptive or a hybrid model.
- Types of life cycles:
  - Predictive- the project scope, time and costs are determined in the early phases of the life cycle. Any changes to the scope are carefully managed. Also called the waterfall method
  - Iterative- the project scope is generally determined early in the project life cycle, but time and cost estimates are routinely modified as the project team's understanding of the product increases
  - Incremental- the deliverable is produced through a series of iterations that successively add functionality within a predetermined time frame
  - Adaptive- agile, iterative or incremental. The detailed scope is defined and approved before the start of an iteration. Also called Agile or change-driven cycles
  - Hybrid- a combination of a predictive and an adaptive life cycle. Those elements of the project that are well known or have fixed requirements follow a predictive development life cycle and those elements that are still evolving follow an adaptive development life cycle

Projectized Organizations

- The entire organizations are organized by projects and project managers are in control of the project
- Project team members in the same office
- Project managers have a high level of independence and authority
- Majority of the organization's resources are involved in project work
- Advantages of a projectized organization

    - Frequent collaboration
    - Rapid decision making
- Disadvantages of a projectized organization
    - Employees working on many projects
    - Idle time
    - Need reassignments

Functional Organizations

- The organization is grouped by specialty. For example there will be a finance department, marketing department, account department, etc.
- Each employee has one clear supervisor to report into
- Each department works separately from other departments. Completes tasks independently
- Advantages of a functional organization
    - Defined Roles
- Disadvantages of a functional organization
    - Lack of communication
    - Lack of collaboration
    - Slow decision making
    - Competing for resources

Matrix Organization

- Blend of both functional and projectized structures

Process Knowledge Areas

Five process groups

1. Initiation
2. Planning
3. Executing
4. Monitoring and Controlling
5. Closing

Ten project management knowledge areas

1. Project Integration Management
2. Project Scope Management
3. Project Schedule Management
4. Project Cost Management
5. Project Quality Management
6. Project Resource Management
7. Project Communications Management
8. Project Risk Management
9. Project Procurement Management
10. Project Stakeholder Management

Key terms in each of the knowledge areas

- Input
    - Any item required before you begin a process
    - Typically they are documents or information
    - It can be internal or external to the project
    - The input for a process is the output from another preceding process

- Tools & Techniques
    - A tool is something tangible. E.g. templates, MS Project. Used to produce a product or result
    - Technique: A systematic procedure that is used to perform and activity within a process. It's a method
    - A single technique may employ more than one tool

- Output
    - A product, result, or service generated by a process
    - The output from one process generally becomes an input to another process or it can be a deliverable of the project

Common Inputs

- Any documents that are key to the process
- Enterprise environment factors
- Organization process assets
- Project management plan
- Work performance information
- Work performance data

Common Tools

- Expert judgment
- Information systems

Common Outputs

- Change Request

INITIATION PROCESS GROUP

- Definition
  - Gives the formal authorization to start a project or phase
  - Clarity to the purpose of a project
  - Identify who has an interest in the project outcome

- Two Processes
  1. Develop project charter
  2. Identify stakeholders

- Two Knowledge Areas
  1. Project Integration Management
  2. Project Stakeholder Management

- Benefits of completing the initiation process
  - Starting a project with objectives
  - Identify a project manager
  - Confirm project viability
  - Manage stakeholders

Planning Process Group

- Definition
  - Define the scope of the project
  - Refine the project objectives
  - Determine the actions to meet objectives
  - Key output is the project management plan
  - All planning is coordinated across the knowledge areas
  - Planning takes place throughout a project, not just the start
  - When there are changes to the project during the planning phase, the scope baseline communications management plan and the risk management plans are updated
  - Updates consolidated into the project management plan

- 24 Processes
  1. Develop Project Management Plan
  2. Plan Scope Management
  3. Collect Requirements
  4. Define Scope
  5. Create WBS
  6. Plan Schedule Management
  7. Define Activities
  8. Sequence Activities
  9. Estimate Activity Resources
  10. Develop Schedule
  11. Plan Cost Management
  12. Estimate Costs
  13. Determine Budget
  14. Plan Quality Management
  15. Plan Resource Management
  16. Estimate Activity Resources
  17. Plan Communications Management
  18. Plan Risk Management
  19. Identify Risks
  20. Perform Qualitative Risk Analysis
  21. Perform Quantitative Risk Analysis
  22. Plan Risk Responses

23. Plan Procurement Management
24. Plan Stakeholder Management

- Ten Knowledge Areas
    1. Project Integration Management
    2. Project Scope Management
    3. Project Schedule Management
    4. Project Cost Management
    5. Project Quality Management
    6. Project Resource Management
    7. Project Communications Management
    8. Project Risk Management
    9. Project Procurement Management
    10. Project Stakeholder Management

Executing Process Group

- Definition
    - The process for carrying out what's in the project management plan
    - Purpose is to complete the work required to meet a project's objectives

- Ten Process Group
    1. Direct and Manage Project Work
    2. Manage Project Knowledge
    3. Managing Quality
    4. Acquire resources
    5. Develop Team
    6. Manage Team
    7. Manage Communications
    8. Implement Risk Responses
    9. Conduct Procurement
    10. Manage Stakeholder Engagement

- Seven Knowledge Areas
    1. Project Integration Management
    2. Project Quality Management
    3. Project Resource Management
    4. Project Communications Management
    5. Project Risk Management
    6. Project Procurement Management
    7. Project Stakeholder Management

Monitoring and Controlling Process Group

- Definition
    - To track progress, review performance, regulate and control variances and change the project management plan if required
    - Includes activities that are key to ensure project compiles with the project management plan. If not, plan needs to be adjusted
    - Performed integrated change control what is used to ensure only approved changes are made to the way the project work is carried

- Twelve Process Groups
    1. Monitor and Control Project Work
    2. Perform Integrated Change Control
    3. Validate Scope
    4. Control Scope
    5. Control Schedule
    6. Control Costs
    7. Control Quality
    8. Control Resource
    9. Monitor Communications
    10. Monitor Risk
    11. Control Procurement
    12. Monitor Stakeholder Engagement

- Ten Knowledge Areas
    1. Project Integration Management
    2. Project Scope Management
    3. Project Schedule Management
    4. Project Cost Management
    5. Project Quality Management
    6. Project Resource Management
    7. Project Communications Management
    8. Project Risk Management
    9. Project Procurement Management
    10. Project Stakeholder Management

CLOSING PROCESS

- Definition
  - To finalize all project activities and formally close a project or phase
  - Conduct phase end or project end reviews
  - Verify acceptance of project deliverables
  - Recording lessons learned
  - Organizational Process Assets Updates

- One Process Groups
  1. Close project or phase

- One Knowledge Areas
  2. Project Integration Management

PROJECT INTEGRATION MANAGEMENT DETAIL

DEVELOP PROJECT CHARTER

- Definition: This formally approves a new project or authorizes a project into its next phase
- Inputs
  - Business Documents: Any sources of information about the project's objectives and how the project will contribute to the business goals.
    - Business case
    - Benefits management plan
  - Agreements: Although it's a document, this will be used as in input if the project is accepted by the external customer and/or client. This can be contracts, memorandums, service level agreements (SLA), letter of intent, verbal agreements, e-mails, etc.
  - Enterprise Environmental Factors: Factors such as culture, internal systems, and procedures, industry standards
  - Organizational Process Assets: Factors such as processes, procedures and corporate knowledge base
- Tools & Techniques
  - Expert Judgment: Expert technical and/or managerial judgment from and qualified sources
  - Data Gathering: Techniques such as brainstorming, focus groups and interviews to gather information
  - Interpersonal and Team Skills: Soft skills such as personality traits, social graces, communication, language, personal habits, friendliness, and optimism that is important to team development
  - Meetings: Discussions with the stakeholders on the progress of the project. Risk management is usually an agenda item
- Outputs
  - Project Charter: A document that authorizes the project and assigns/authorizes the project manager
  - Assumption: A factor in the planning process that is considered to be true, real, or certain, without proof or demonstration.

Develop Project Management Plan

- Definition: Documenting all actions required to define, prepare and coordinate all plan components and consolidating them into an integrated project management plan
- Inputs
    - Project Charter: A document that authorizes the project and assigns/authorizes the project manager
    - Outputs from other processes: Subsidiary plans and baselines that are an output from other processes are inputs to this process
    - Enterprise Environmental Factors: Factors such as culture, internal systems, and procedures, industry standards
    - Organizational Process Assets: Factors such as processes, procedures and corporate knowledge base
- Tools & Techniques
    - Expert Judgment: Expert technical and/or managerial judgment from and qualified sources
    - Data Gathering: Techniques such as brainstorming, focus groups and interviews to gather information
    - Interpersonal and Team Skills: Soft skills such as personality traits, social graces, communication, language, personal habits, friendliness, and optimism that is important to team development
    - Meetings: Discussions with the stakeholders on the progress of the project. Risk management is usually an agenda item
- Outputs
    - Project Management Plan: All of the management plans and the baselines together in one document

Direct and Manage Project Work

- Definition: Executes the work defined in the project management plan
- Inputs
    - Project Management Plan: All of the management plans and the baselines together in one document
        - Any components
    - Project Documents: Any project documents that may need to be updated
        - Change log
        - Lessons learned register
        - Milestone list
        - Project communications
        - Project schedule
        - Requirements traceability matrix
        - Risk register
        - Risk report
    - Approved Change Requests: A documentation that shows all authorized changes that expand or reduce scope
    - Enterprise Environmental Factors: Factors such as culture, internal systems, and procedures, industry standard
    - Organizational Process Assets: Factors such as processes, procedures and corporate knowledge base
- Tools & Techniques
    - Expert Judgment: Expert technical and/or managerial judgment from and qualified sources
    - Project Management Information System (PMIS): Automated system to help the team execute planned activities
    - Meetings: Used to discuss and address topics that are related to the project. Attendees can include the project team and stakeholders. Meetings can occur in person or virtually
- Outputs
    - Deliverables: A tangible (such as a product) or intangible (such as a service) of activities performed

- Work Performance Data: The data that relates to the status, schedule progress, and costs incurred
- Issue Log: Written log that lists specific issues, who owns the issue and dates when the issue will be resolved
- Change Requests: Requests for changes to scope, schedule, costs, processes or other project documentation.
- Project Management Plan Updates: Any updates to the Project Management Plan as a result of this process
    - Any components
- Project Documents Updates: Any updates that are made to the above documents
    - Activity list
    - Assumption log
    - Lessons learned register
    - Requirements documentation
    - risk register
    - Stakeholder register
- Organizational Process Assets Updates: Updates to Updates to documents such as guidelines, procedures, historical information that is related to the organization

Manage Project Knowledge

- Definition: Using existing knowledge and creating new knowledge to achieve the project's objectives and contribute to organizational learning
- Inputs
  - Project Management Plan: All of the management plans and the baselines together in one document
    - All components
  - Project Documents: Any project documents that may need to be updated
    - Lessons learned register
    - Project team assignments
    - Resource breakdown structure
    - Source selection criteria
    - Stakeholder register
  - Deliverables: A tangible (such as a product) or intangible (such as a service) of activities performed
  - Enterprise Environmental Factors: Factors such as culture, internal systems, and procedures, industry standard
  - Organizational Process Assets: Factors such as processes, procedures and corporate knowledge base
- Tools & Techniques
  - Expert Judgment: Expert technical and/or managerial judgment from and qualified sources
  - Knowledge Management: Tools and techniques that connect people so they can work together to create new knowledge, share tacit knowledge, and integrate the knowledge of diverse team members. Some examples are workshops, training, and networking
  - Information Management: Tools and techniques that are used to create and connect people to information for sharing simple, unambiguous, codified explicit knowledge
  - Interpersonal and Team Skills: Soft skills such as personality traits, social graces, communication, language, personal habits, friendliness, and optimism that is important to team development
- Outputs

- Lessons Learned Register: Contains the impact, recommendations and proposed actions associated with situations during the life of a project. It may record challenges, problems, realized risks, and opportunities or other content as appropriate
- Project Management Plan: All of the management plans and the baselines together in one document
  - Any component

MONITOR AND CONTROL PROJECT WORK

- Definition: Monitors the work defined in the project management plan by continuously reviewing the performance of the project through collecting and measuring the trends that may affect the project.
- Inputs
  - Project Management Plan: All of the management plans and the baselines together in one document
    - Any Component
  - Project Documents: Any project documents that may need to be updated
    - Assumptions log
    - Basis of estimates
    - Cost forecasts
    - Issues log
    - Lessons learned register
    - Milestone list
    - Quality reports
    - Risk register
    - Risk report
    - Schedule forecasts
  - Work Performance Information: The data that relates to the status, schedule progress, and costs incurred
  - Enterprise Environmental Factors: Factors such as culture, internal systems, and procedures, industry standard
  - Organizational Process Assets: Factors such as processes, procedures and corporate knowledge base

- Tools & Techniques
    - Expert Judgment: Expert technical and/or managerial judgment from and qualified sources
    - Data Analysis: Using techniques such as alternative analysis, cost-benefit analysis, trend analysis and variance analysis to make decisions on the project
    - Decision Making: The action or process of making decisions, especially important ones
    - Meetings: Used to discuss and address topics that are related to the project. Attendees can include the project team and stakeholders. Meetings can occur in person or virtually
- Outputs
    - Work Performance Reports: Actual documentation the represents the work performance information compiled in project documents
    - Change Requests: Requests for changes to scope, schedule, costs, processes or other project documentation
    - Project Management Plan Updates: Any updates to the Project Management Plan as a result of this process
        - Any component
    - Project Documents Updates: Any updates that are made to the above documents
        - Cost forecasts
        - Issues log
        - Lessons learned register
        - Risk register
        - Schedule forecasts

Perform Integrated Change Control

- Definition: Reviewing and approving change requests, then managing the changes to the deliverables, documentation, and assets
- Inputs
    - Project Management Plan: All of the management plans and the baselines together in one document
        - Change management plan
        - Configure management plan
        - Scope baseline

        - Schedule baseline
        - Cost baseline
    - Project Documents: Any project documents that may need to be updated
        - Basis of estimates
        - Requirements traceability matrix
        - Risk report
    - Work Performance Reports: Actual documentation the represents the work performance information compiled in project documents
    - Change Requests: Requests for changes to scope, schedule, costs, processes or other project documentation.
    - Enterprise Environmental Factors: Factors such as culture, internal systems, and procedures, industry standards
    - Organizational Process Assets: Factors such as processes, procedures and corporate knowledge base
- Tools & Techniques
    - Expert Judgment: Expert technical and/or managerial judgment from and qualified sources
    - Change Control Tools: Automated tools used to manage change requests and the resulting decisions
    - Data Analysis: Using techniques such as alternative analysis, cost-benefit analysis, trend analysis and variance analysis to make decisions on the project
    - Decision Making: The action or process of making decisions, especially important ones
    - Meetings: Used to discuss and address topics that are related to the project. Attendees can include the project team and stakeholders. Meetings can occur in person or virtually
- Outputs
    - Approved Change Requests: A documentation that shows all authorized changes that expand or reduce scope
    - Project Management Plan Updates: Any updates to the Project Management Plan as a result of this process
        - Any components
    - Project Documents Updates: Any updates that are made to the above documents
        - Change log

Close Project or Phase

- Definition: Formally closes the project, project phase or contract
- Inputs
    - Project Charter: A document that authorizes the project and assigns/authorizes the project manager
    - Project Management Plan: All of the management plans and the baselines together in one document
        - All components
    - Project Documents: Project documents that may need to be updated
        - Assumption log
        - Basis of estimates
        - Change log
        - Issue log
        - Lessons learned register
        - Milestone list
        - Project communications
        - Quality control measurements
        - Quality reports
        - Requirements documentation
        - Risk register
        - Risk report
    - Accepted Deliverables: A list of all deliverables that have been accepted from the Validate scope process
    - Business Documents: Any sources of information about the project's objectives and how the project will contribute to the business goals
        - Business case
        - Benefits management plan
    - Agreements: Any document or communication that defines the initial intentions of a project. This can take the form of a contract, memo, verbal agreements, email, etc.

    - Procurement Documentation: Used to demonstrate compliance with the project scope
    - Organizational Process Assets: Factors such as processes, procedures and corporate knowledge base
- Tools & Techniques
    - Expert Judgment: Expert technical and/or managerial judgment from and qualified sources
    - Data Analysis: Using techniques such as alternative analysis, cost-benefit analysis, trend analysis and variance analysis to make decisions on the project
    - Meetings: Used to discuss and address topics that are related to the project. Attendees can include the project team and stakeholders. Meetings can occur in person or virtually
- Outputs
    - Project Documents Updates: Any updates that are made to the above documents
        - Lessons learned register
    - Final Product, Service or Result Transition: The final product, service or what results of the project or project phase
    - Final Report: Provides a summary of the project performance. It can include information such as summary level description of the project or phase, scope objectives, quality objectives, cost objectives and summary of the validation information for the final product, service or result
    - Organizational Process Assets Updates: Updates to documents such as guidelines, procedures, historical information that is related to the organization

PROJECT SCOPE MANAGEMENT DETAILS

PLAN SCOPE MANAGEMENT

- Definition: Documents how the scope will be defined developed, monitored, controlled and verified. This helps reduce project scope creep
- Inputs
    - Project Charter: A document that authorizes the project and assigns/authorizes the project manager
    - Project Management Plan: All of the management plans and the baselines together in one document
        - Quality management plan
        - Project life cycle description
        - Development approach
    - Enterprise Environmental Factors: Factors such as culture, internal systems, and procedures, industry standards
    - Organizational Process Assets: Factors such as processes, procedures and corporate knowledge base
- Tools & Techniques
    - Expert Judgment: Expert technical and/or managerial judgment from and qualified sources
    - Data Analysis: Using techniques such as alternative analysis, cost-benefit analysis, trend analysis and variance analysis to make decisions on the project
    - Meetings: Used to discuss and address topics that are related to the project. Attendees can include the project team and stakeholders. Meetings can occur in person or virtually
- Outputs
    - Scope Management Plan: A document that lists out how the scope will be defined, developed, monitored, controlled and verified
    - Requirements Management Plan: A document on how requirements will be reviewed, recorded and managed

Collect Requirement

- Definition: Defines and documents the project and product features and functions needed to fill stakeholders needs and expectations
- Inputs
    - Project Charter: A document that authorizes the project and assigns/authorizes the project manager
    - Project Management Plan: All of the management plans and the baselines together in one document
        - Scope management plan
        - Requirements management plan
        - Stakeholder engagement plan
    - Project Documents: Project documents that may need to be updated
        - Assumptions log
        - Lessons learned register
        - Stakeholder register
    - Business Documents: Any sources of information about the project's objectives and how the project will contribute to the business goals.
        - Business case
    - Agreements: Any document or communication that defines the initial intentions of a project. This can take the form of a contract, memo, verbal baseline, email, etc.
    - Enterprise Environmental Factors: Factors such as culture, internal systems, and procedures, industry standard
    - Organizational Process Assets: Factors such as processes, procedures and corporate knowledge base
- Tools & Techniques
    - Expert Judgment: Expert technical and/or managerial judgment from and qualified sources
    - Data Gathering: Techniques such as brainstorming, focus groups, and interviews to gather information.
    - Data Analysis: Using techniques such as alternative analysis, cost-benefit analysis, trend analysis and variance analysis to make decisions on the project
    - Decision Making: The action or process of making decisions, especially important ones.

- Data Representation: Techniques such as affinity diagrams and mind mapping to organize ideas in order to generate new ones.
- Interpersonal and Team Skills: Soft skills such as personality traits, social graces, communication, language, personal habits, friendliness, and optimism that is important to team development
- Context diagrams: Shows the scope and business system (process, equipment, computer system, etc.) visually and how they interact with each other
- Prototypes: Creating a model of a product and using it for research before actually creating the product for mass production.

- Outputs
  - Requirements Documentation: A document that describes how each requirement meet the business needs of the project
  - Requirements Traceability Matrix: A document that lists the requirements for when they were created and follows them throughout the project

Define Scope

- Definition: This formally approves a new project or authorizes a project into its next phase
- Inputs
  - Project Charter: A document that authorizes the project and assigns/authorizes the project manager
  - Project Management Plan: All of the management plans and the baselines together in one document
    - Scope management plan
  - Project Documents: Project documents that may need to be updated
    - Assumption log
    - Requirements documentation
    - Risk register
  - Enterprise Environmental Factors: Factors such as culture, internal systems, and procedures, industry standard
  - Organizational Process Assets: Factors such as processes, procedures and corporate knowledge base
- Tools & Techniques

  - Expert Judgment: Expert technical and/or managerial judgment from and qualified sources
  - Data Analysis: Using techniques such as alternative analysis, cost-benefit analysis, trend analysis and variance analysis to make decisions on the project
  - Decision Making: The action or process of making decisions, especially important ones.
  - Interpersonal and Team Skills: Soft skills such as personality traits, social graces, communication, language, personal habits, friendliness, and optimism that is important to team development
  - Product Analysis: Method for translating high-level product descriptions into tangible deliverables that use techniques such as a product breakdown, systems analysis, and requirements analysis
- Outputs
  - Project Scope Statement: A document that lists out the project deliverables and what it takes to deliver them
  - Project Documents Updates: Any updates that are made to the above documents
    - Assumptions log
    - Requirements documentation
    - Requirements traceability matrix
    - Stakeholder register

CREATE WBS

- Definition: Subdivides major deliverables into manageable components
- Inputs
  - Project Management Plan: All of the management plans and the baselines together in one document
    - Scope management plan
  - Project Documents: Any project documents that may need to be updated
    - Project scope statement
    - Requirements documentation
  - Enterprise Environmental Factors: Factors such as culture, internal systems, and procedures, industry standards
  - Organizational Process Assets: Factors such as processes, procedures and corporate knowledge base
- Tools & Techniques

    - Expert Judgment: Expert technical and/or managerial judgment from and qualified sources
    - Decomposition: Dividing the deliverables into smaller workable packages that resources can execute against.
- Outputs
    - Scope Baseline: The approved project scope statement, the WBS, and the WBS dictionary
    - Project Documents Updates: Any updates that are made to the above documents
        - Assumption log
        - Requirements documentation

VALIDATE SCOPE

- Definition: Formalizes acceptance of completed project deliverables
- Inputs
    - Project Management Plan: all of the management plans and the baselines together in one document
        - Scope management plan
        - Requirements management plan
        - Scope baseline
    - Project Documents: Project documents that may need to be updated
        - Lessons learned register
        - Quality reports
        - Requirements documentation
        - Requirements traceability matrix
    - Verified Deliverables: Deliverables that have been completed using the Control Quality process
    - Work Performance Data: The data that relates to the status, schedule progress, and costs incurred
- Tools & Techniques
    - Inspection: An examination to ensure the end results are to expected requirements. Could be done through an audit, walkthrough or formal review.
    - Decision Making: The action or process of making decisions, especially important ones
- Outputs

- Accepted Deliverables: A list of all deliverables that have been accepted from the Validate scope process
- Work Performance Information: The actual raw data use used to deliver status, schedule, and cost of the project
- Change Requests: Requests for changes to scope, schedule, costs, processes or other project documentation
- Project Documents Updates: Any updates that are made to the above documents
  - Lessons learned register
  - Requirements documentation
  - Requirements traceability matrix

Control Scope

- Definition: Controls changes to project scope
- Inputs
  - Project Management Plan: all of the management plans and the baselines together in one document
    - Scope management plan
    - Requirements management plan
    - Change management plan
    - Configuration management plan
    - Scope baseline
    - Performance measurement baseline
  - Project Documents: Project documents that may need to be updated
    - Lessons learned register
    - Requirements documentation
    - Requirements traceability matrix
  - Work Performance Data: The data that relates to the status, schedule progress, and costs incurred
  - Organizational Process Assets: Factors such as processes, procedures and corporate knowledge base
- Tools & Techniques
  - Data Analysis: Using techniques such as alternative analysis, cost-benefit analysis, trend analysis and variance analysis to make decisions on the project

- Outputs
    - Work Performance Information: The actual raw data use used to deliver status, schedule, and cost of the project
    - Change Requests: Requests for changes to scope, schedule, costs, processes or other project documentation
    - Project Management Plan Updates: Any updates to the Project Management Plan as a result of this process
        - Scope management plan
        - Scope baseline
        - Schedule baseline
        - Cost baseline
        - Performance measurement baseline
    - Project Document Updates: Updates to other project documentation
        - Lessons learned register
        - Requirements documentation
        - Requirements traceability matrix

Project Schedule Management Details

Plan Schedule Management

- Definition: Establishing the policies, procedures, and documentation for planning developing, managing, executing and controlling the program
- Inputs:
    - Project Charter: A document that authorizes the project and assigns/authorizes the project manager
    - Project Management Plan: All of the management plans and the baselines together in one document
        - Scope management plan
        - Development approach
    - Enterprise Environmental Factors: Factors such as culture, internal systems, and procedures, industry standards
    - Organizational Process Assets: Factors such as processes, procedures and corporate knowledge base
- Tools & Techniques
    - Expert Judgment: Expert technical and/or managerial judgment from and qualified sources
    - Data Analysis: Using techniques such as alternative analysis, cost-benefit analysis, trend analysis and variance analysis to make decisions on the project
    - Meetings: Used to discuss and address topics that are related to the project. Attendees can include the project team and stakeholders. Meetings can occur in person or virtually
- Outputs
    - Schedule Management Plan: Details how if the project schedule changes, how it will be managed

DEFINE ACTIVITIES

- Definition: The process of specifically identifying all scheduled actions to be performed to produce the project deliverables
- Inputs
    - Project Management Plan: All of the management plans and the baselines together in one document
        - Schedule management plan
        - Scope baseline
    - Enterprise Environmental Factors: Factors such as culture, internal systems, and procedures, industry standards
    - Organizational Process Assets: Factors such as processes, procedures and corporate knowledge base
- Tools & Techniques
    - Expert Judgment: Expert technical and/or managerial judgment from and qualified sources
    - Decomposition: Dividing the deliverables into smaller workable packages that resources can execute against.
    - Rolling Wave Planning: Planning in phases instead of the entire project upfront
    - Meeting: Discussions with the stakeholders on the progress of the project. Risk management is usually an agenda item
- Outputs
    - Activity List: The complete list and description of all activities
    - Activity Attributes: Gives each of the activities in the activity list a description of what is being done
    - Milestone List: A schedule list that shows dates of when activities are due
    - Change Requests: Requests for changes to scope, schedule, costs, processes or other project documentation
    - Project Management Plan Updates: Any updates to the Project Management Plan as a result of this process
        - Schedule baseline
        - Cost baseline

SEQUENCE ACTIVITIES

- Definition: Identifies and documents dependencies among scheduled activities
- Inputs
    - Project Management Plan: All of the management plans and the baselines together in one document
        - Schedule management plan
        - Scope baseline
    - Project Documents: Project documents that may need to be updated
        - Activity attributes
        - Activity list
        - Assumption log
        - Milestone list
    - Enterprise Environmental Factors: Factors such as culture, internal systems, and procedures, industry standard
    - Organizational Process Assets: Factors such as processes, procedures and corporate knowledge base
- Tools & Techniques
    - Precedence Diagramming Method (PMD): Activity-on-Node (AON) project network diagramming method
    - Dependency Determination: Mandatory dependencies, discretionary dependencies, external dependencies
    - Leads and Lags: Refining the schedule by adjusting the start time of linked activities without impacting resources
    - Project Management Information Systems (PMIS): Includes scheduling software that has the capability to help plan, organize projects
- Outputs
    - Project Schedule Network Diagrams: Schematic displays of the project's activities and their logical relationships
    - Project Documents Updates: Any updates that are made to the above documents
        - Activity attributes
        - Activity list
        - Assumption log

        - Milestone list

ESTIMATE ACTIVITY DURATIONS

- Definition: Estimates the number of work periods for each scheduled activity
- Inputs
    - Project Management Plan: All of the management plans and the baselines together in one document
        - Schedule management baseline
        - Scope baseline
    - Project Documents: Project documents that may need to be updated
        - Activity attributes
        - Activity list
        - Assumption log
        - Lessons learned register
        - Milestone list
        - Project team assignments
        - Resource breakdown structure
        - Resource requirements
        - Risk register
    - Enterprise Environmental Factors: Factors such as culture, internal systems, and procedures, industry standard
    - Organizational Process Assets: Factors such as processes, procedures and corporate knowledge base
- Tools & Techniques
    - Expert Judgment: Expert technical and/or managerial judgment from and qualified sources
    - Analogous Estimating: Using previous projects to base current estimates
    - Parametric Analysis: Use of project 'parameters' to calculate predicted durations
    - Three-Point Estimates: Creating three estimates- most likely, optimistic and pessimistic estimates to make an overall forecasted estimate
    - Bottom-Up Estimating: Estimating individual activities, then rolling-up the summary to calculate your project
    - Data Analysis: Using techniques such as alternative analysis, cost-benefit analysis, trend analysis and variance analysis to make decisions on the project

- Decision Making: The action or process of making decisions, especially important ones
- Meeting: Discussions with the stakeholders on the progress of the project. Risk management is usually an agenda item

- Output
  - Duration Estimates: Estimate time to complete each scheduled activity
  - Basis of Estimates: A Document that shows the costs estimates by providing information on how the estimates were calculated such as assumptions, constraints, level of detail, ranges, and confidence levels
  - Project Documents Updates: Any updates that are made to the above documents
    - Activity attributes
    - Assumption log
    - Lessons learned register

Develop Schedule

- Definition: Analyzes activity sequences, durations, resource requirements, and schedule constraints to create the project schedule model for project execution and monitoring and controlling
- Inputs
  - Project Management Plan: All of the management plans and the baselines together in one document
    - Schedule management plan
    - Scope baseline
  - Project Documents: Project documents that may need to be updated
    - Activity attributes
    - Activity list
    - Assumption log
    - Basis of estimates
    - Duration estimates
    - Lessons learned register
    - Milestone list
    - Project schedule network diagrams

        - Project team assignments
        - Resource calendars
        - Resource requirements
        - Risk register
    - Agreements: Any document or communication that defines the initial intentions of a project. This can take the form of a contract, memo, verbal agreements, email, etc.
    - Enterprise Environmental Factors: Factors such as culture, internal systems, and procedures, industry standard
    - Organizational Process Assets: Factors such as processes, procedures and corporate knowledge base
- Tools & Techniques
    - Schedule Network Analysis: Method that creates the project schedule, and uses different schedule models
    - Critical Path Method: Calculates schedule dates and the absolute path that needs to be taken to complete the project or phase
    - Resource Optimization Techniques: Creates efficiencies for schedules that have limited resource such as using resource leveling and resource smoothing
    - Data Analysis: Using techniques such as alternative analysis, cost-benefit analysis, trend analysis and variance analysis to make decisions on the project
    - Leads and Lags: Refining the schedule by adjusting the start time of linked activities without impacting resources
    - Schedule Compression: Also called “fast-tracking” and “crashing”, it shortens the schedule of the project without changing the scope
    - Project Management Information Systems (PMIS): Includes scheduling software that has the capability to help plan, organize projects
    - Agile Release Planning: A high-level summary timeline of the release schedule based on the product roadmap and the product vision for the product's evolution
- Output
    - Schedule Baseline: Specific version of the project schedule, accepted by the team as the project’s schedule baseline
    - Project Schedule: A document that outlines the start and finish dates for each project activity
    - Schedule Data: The schedule milestones, activities, activities, and all documented assumptions and constraints

- Project Calendars: Identifies the working days and times on which resources can complete activities
- Change Requests: Requests for changes to scope, schedule, costs, processes or other project documentation
- Project Management Plan Updates: Any updates to the Project Management Plan as a result of this process
  - Schedule management plan
  - Cost baseline
- Project Documents Updates: Any updates that are made to the above documents
  - Activity attributes
  - Assumption log
  - Duration estimates
  - Lessons learned register
  - Resource requirements
  - Risk register

Control Schedule

- Definition: Monitoring the status of the project to update the project schedule and manage changes to the schedule baseline.
- Inputs
  - Project Management Plan: All of the management plans and the baselines together in one document
    - Schedule management plan
    - Schedule baseline
    - Scope baseline
    - Performance measurement baseline
  - Project Documents: Project documents that may need to be updated
    - Lessons learned register
    - Project calendars
    - Project schedule
    - Resource calendar
    - Schedule data

- Work Performance Data: The data that relates to the status, schedule progress, and costs incurred
- Organizational Process Assets: Factors such as processes, procedures and corporate knowledge base

- Tools & Techniques
  - Data Analysis: Using techniques such as alternative analysis, cost-benefit analysis, trend analysis and variance analysis to make decisions on the project
  - Critical Path Method: Calculates schedule dates and the absolute path that needs to be taken to complete the project or phase
  - Project Management Information Systems (PMIS): Includes scheduling software that has the capability to help plan, organize projects
  - Resource Optimization Techniques: Creates efficiencies for schedules that have limited resource such as using resource leveling and resource smoothing
  - Leads and Lags: Refining the schedule by adjusting the start time of linked activities without impacting resources
  - Schedule Compression: Also called "fast-tracking" and "crashing", it shortens the schedule of the project without changing the scope
- Outputs
  - Work Performance Information: The actual raw data use used to deliver status, schedule, and cost of the project
  - Schedule Forecast: Used to determine the time estimated to complete work, computed as estimates to complete (ETC). Expressed in terms of schedule variance (SV) and schedule performance index (SPI)
  - Change Requests: Requests for changes to scope, schedule, costs, processes or other project documentation.
  - Project Management Plan Updates: Any updates to the Project Management Plan as a result of this process
    - Schedule management plan
    - Schedule baseline
    - Cost baseline
    - Performance measurement baseline
  - Project Documents Updates: Any updates that are made to the above documents
    - Assumption log
    - Basis of estimates

- Lessons learned register
- Project schedule
- Resource calendars
- Risk register
- Schedule data

Project Cost Management Details

Plan Cost Management

- Definition: The process of defining how the project costs will be estimated, budgeted, managed, monitored a
- Inputs
    - Project Charter: A document that authorizes the project and assigns/authorizes the project manager
    - Project Management Plan: All of the management plans and the baselines together in one document
        - Schedule management plan
        - Risk management plan
    - Enterprise Environmental Factors: Factors such as culture, internal systems, and procedures, industry standard
    - Organizational Process Assets: Factors such as processes, procedures and corporate knowledge base
- Tools & Techniques
    - Expert Judgment: Expert technical and/or managerial judgment from and qualified sources
    - Data Analysis: Using techniques such as alternative analysis, cost-benefit analysis, trend analysis and variance analysis to make decisions on the project
    - Meetings: A meeting with the stakeholders to develop a plan to manage risks
- Outputs
    - Cost Management Plan: It details how the following should be managed: risk budgets, contingencies, and reserves

Estimate Costs

- Definition: Approximating the cost of resources needed to complete project work
- Input
    - Project Management Plan: All of the management plans and the baselines together in one document
        - Cost management plan

        - Quality management plan
        - Scope baseline
    - Project Documents: Project documents that may need to be updated
        - Lessons learned register
        - Project schedule
        - Resources requirements
        - Risk Register
    - Enterprise Environmental Factors: Factors such as culture, internal systems, and procedures, industry standard
    - Organizational Process Assets: Factors such as processes, procedures and corporate knowledge base
- Tools & Techniques
    - Expert Judgment: Expert technical and/or managerial judgment from and qualified sources
    - Analogous Estimating: Using previous projects to base current estimates
    - Parametric Analysis: Use of project 'parameters' to calculate predicted durations
    - Bottom-Up Estimate: Create an estimate by preparing the lower, detailed work then aggregating into the total quantity of the activity
    - Three-Point Estimates: Creating three estimates: most likely (C_M), optimistic(C_O) and pessimistic (C_P)estimates to make an overall forecasted estimate
        - Note: PERT analysis calculation is expected (C_E) activity cost using a weighted average of the three estimates: $C_E = C_O + 4C_M + C_P/6$
    - Data Analysis: Using techniques such as alternative analysis, cost-benefit analysis, trend analysis and variance analysis to make decisions on the project
    - Project Management Information Systems (PMIS): Includes scheduling software that has the capability to help plan, organize projects
    - Decision Making: The action or process of making decisions, especially important ones
- Output
    - Cost Estimates: Quantitative assessments of the probable costs required to complete project work, as well as contingency amounts to cover unplanned work
    - Basis of Estimates: A Document that shows the costs estimates by providing information on how the estimates were calculated
    - Project Documents Updates: Any updates that are made to the above documents
        - Assumption log

        - Lessons learned register
        - Risk register

Determine Budget

- Definition: Aggregating the estimated costs of individual activities or work packages to establish an authorized cost baseline
- Inputs
    - Project Management Plan: All of the management plans and the baselines together in one document
        - Cost management plan
        - Resource management plan
        - Scope baseline
    - Project Documents: Project documents that may need to be updated
        - Basis of estimates
        - Cost estimates
        - Project schedule
        - Risk register
    - Business Documents: Any sources of information about the project's objectives and how the project will contribute to the business goals.
        - Business case
        - Benefits management plan
    - Agreements: Applicable contracts or agreement information for products and services to be purchased from external sources
    - Enterprise Environmental Factors: Factors such as culture, internal systems, and procedures, industry standard
    - Organizational Process Assets: Factors such as processes, procedures and corporate knowledge base
- Tools & Techniques
    - Expert Judgment: Expert technical and/or managerial judgment from and qualified sources
    - Cost Aggregation: Gathering scheduled activity cost estimates by work packages
    - Data Analysis: Using techniques such as alternative analysis, cost-benefit analysis, trend analysis and variance analysis to make decisions on the project

    - Historical Relationships: Two models used for cost estimation: Analogous and Parametric
    - Funding Limit Reconciliation: In order to avoid large variations in sporadic expenses, schedules need to be adjusted
    - Financing: Acquiring funding for projects. Sources of funding could come from internally or externally.
- Outputs
    - Cost Baseline: The approved version of the time-phased budget. It is used as a basis for comparison to actual results
    - Project Funding Requirements: Define the funding needed and when it will be needed
    - Project Documents Updates: Any updates that are made to the above documents
        - Cost estimates
        - Project schedule
        - Risk register

CONTROL COSTS

- Definition: Monitoring the status of the project to update the project costs and manage changes to the cost baseline
- Inputs
    - Project Management Plan: all of the management plans and the baselines together in one document
        - Cost management plan
        - Cost baseline
        - Performance measurement baseline
    - Project Documents: Any project documents that may need to be updated
        - Lessons learned register
    - Project Funding Requirements: Define the funding needed and when it will be needed
    - Work Performance Data: The data that relates to the status, schedule progress, and costs incurred
    - Organizational Process Assets: Factors such as processes, procedures and corporate knowledge base

- Tools & Techniques
    - Expert Judgment: Expert technical and/or managerial judgment from and qualified sources
    - Data Analysis: Using techniques such as alternative analysis, cost-benefit analysis, trend analysis and variance analysis to make decisions on the project
    - To-Complete Performance Index (TCPI): The projection of the anticipated performance required to achieve management's goal
    - Project Management Information Systems (PMIS): Includes scheduling software that has the capability to help plan, organize projects
- Outputs
    - Work Performance Information: The actual raw data use used to deliver status, schedule, and cost of the project
    - Cost Forecast: Used to estimate how much it will cost to complete work, computed as estimates to complete (ETC). Expressed in terms of cost variance (CV) and cost performance index (CPI)
    - Change Requests: Requests for changes to scope, schedule, costs, processes or other project documentation
    - Project Management Plan Updates: Any updates to the Project Management Plan as a result of this process
        - Cost management plan
        - Cost baseline
        - Performance measurement baseline
    - Project Documents Updates: Any updates that are made to the above documents
        - Assumption log
        - Basis of estimates
        - Cost estimates
        - Lessons learned register
        - Risk register

PROJECT QUALITY MANAGEMENT DETAILS

PLAN QUALITY MANAGEMENT

- Definition: Identifies project quality requirements and/or standards for the project and its deliverables, and documenting how the project will demonstrate compliance with quality requirements and/or standards
- Inputs
    - Project Charter: A document that authorizes the project and assigns/authorizes the project manager
    - Project Management Plan: All of the management plans and the baselines together in one document
        - Requirements management plan
        - Risk management plan
        - Stakeholder engagement plan
        - Scope baseline
    - Project Documents: Any project documents that may need to be updated
        - Assumption log
        - Requirements documentation
        - Requirements traceability matrix
    - Enterprise Environmental Factors: Factors such as culture, internal systems, and procedures, industry standard
    - Organizational Process Assets: Factors such as processes, procedures and corporate knowledge base
- Tools & Techniques
    - Expert Judgment: Expert technical and/or managerial judgment from and qualified sources
    - Data Gathering: Techniques such as brainstorming, focus groups and interviews to gather information
    - Data Analysis: Using techniques such as alternative analysis, cost-benefit analysis, trend analysis and variance analysis to make decisions on the project
    - Decision Making: The action or process of making decisions, especially important ones
    - Data Representation: Techniques such as affinity diagrams and mind mapping to organize ideas in order to generate new ones.

    - Test and Inspection Planning: Project team determines how to test or inspect the product, deliverable, or service to meet the stakeholders' needs and expectation, as well as how to meet the goal for the product's performance and reliability
    - Meetings: Used to discuss and address topics that are related to the project. Attendees can include the project team and stakeholders. Meetings can occur in person or virtually
- Outputs
    - Quality Management Plan: Describes how the team will implement the organization's quality policy
    - Quality Metrics: Operational definitions, project elements and how they are to be measured by quality control
    - Project Management Plan Updates: Any updates to the Project Management Plan as a result of this process
        - Risk management plan
        - Scope baseline
    - Project Documents Updates: Any updates that are made to the above documents
        - Lessons learned register
        - Requirements traceability matrix
        - Risk register
        - Stakeholder register

MANAGE QUALITY

- Definition: Translating the quality management plan into executable quality activities that incorporate the organization's quality policies into the project
- Inputs
    - Project Management Plan: All of the management plans and the baselines together in one document
        - Quality management plan
    - Project Documents: Project documents that may need to be updated
        - Lessons learned register
        - Quality control measurement
        - Quality metrics
        - Risk report
    - Organizational Process Assets: Factors such as processes, procedures and corporate knowledge base

- Tools & Techniques
  - Data Gathering: Techniques such as brainstorming, focus groups and interviews to gather information
  - Data Analysis: Using techniques such as alternative analysis, cost-benefit analysis, trend analysis and variance analysis to make decisions on the project
  - Decision Making: The action or process of making decisions, especially important ones
  - Data Representation: Techniques such as affinity diagrams and mind mapping to organize ideas in order to generate new ones.
  - Audits: Structured, independent process used to determine if project activities comply with organizational and project policies, processes and procedure
  - Design for X (DfX): A set of technical guidelines that may be applied during the design of a product for the optimization of a specific aspect of the design. This can control or even improve the product's final characteristics
  - Problem Solving: Entails finding solutions for issues or challenges. It can include gathering additional information, critical thinking, creative, quantitative and/or logical approaches.
  - Quality Improvement Methods: Tools such as Plan-do-check-act and Six Sigma are used to analyze and evaluate opportunities for improvement
- Outputs
  - Quality Reports: Information about quality that is either graphical, numerical, or qualitative, can be used by other processes and departments to take corrective actions in order to achieve the project quality expectations
  - Test and Evaluation Documents: Created based on industry needs and the organization's template to evaluate the achievement of quality objectives
  - Change Requests: Requests for changes to scope, schedule, costs, processes or other project documentation
  - Project Management Plan Updates: Any updates to the Project Management Plan as a result of this process
    - Quality management plan
    - Scope baseline
    - Schedule baseline
    - Cost baseline
  - Project Documents Updates: Any updates that are made to the above documents
    - Issue log
    - Lessons learned register

- Risk register

CONTROL QUALITY

- Definition: Monitoring and recording the results of the executing the quality management activities to assess performance and ensure the project outputs are complete, correct and meet customer expectation
  - Inputs
    - Project Management Plan: All of the management plans and the baselines together in one document
      - Quality management plan
    - Project Documents: Project documents that may need to be updated
      - Lessons learned register
      - Quality metrics
      - Test and evaluation documents
    - Approved Change Requests: A documentation that shows all authorized changes that expand or reduce scope
    - Deliverables: A tangible (such as a product) or intangible (such as a service) of activities performed
    - Work Performance Data: The data that relates to the status, schedule progress, and costs incurred
    - Enterprise Environmental Factors: Factors such as culture, internal systems and procedures, industry standard
    - Organizational Process Assets: Factors such as processes, procedures and corporate knowledge base
  - Tools & Techniques
    - Data Gathering: Techniques such as brainstorming, focus groups and interviews to gather information
    - Data Analysis: Using techniques such as alternative analysis, cost-benefit analysis, trend analysis and variance analysis to make decisions on the project
    - Inspection: An examination to ensure the end results are to expected requirements. Could be done through an audit, walkthrough or formal review.
    - Testing/Product Evaluations: An organized and constructed investigation conducted to provide objective information about the quality of the product or service under test in accordance with the project requirements to find errors, defects, bugs or other non-conformance problems in the product or service

    - Data Representation: Techniques such as affinity diagrams and mind mapping to organize ideas in order to generate new ones.
    - Meeting: Discussions with the stakeholders on the progress of the project. Risk management is usually an agenda item
- Outputs
    - Quality Control Measurements: The results of the quality control activities
    - Verified Deliverables: Deliverables that have been completed using the Control Quality process
    - Work Performance Information: The actual raw data use used to deliver status, schedule, and cost of the project
    - Change Requests: Requests for changes to scope, schedule, costs, processes or other project documentation.
    - Project Management Plan Updates: Any updates to the Project Management Plan as a result of this process
        - Quality management plan
    - Project Documents Updates: Any updates that are made to the above documents
        - Issues log
        - Lessons learned register
        - Risk Register
        - Test and evaluation documents

Project Resource Management Details

Plan Resource Management

- Definition: Defining how to estimate, acquire, manage, and utilize physical and team resources
- Inputs
    - Project Charter: A document that authorizes the project and assigns/authorizes the project manager
    - Project Management Plan: All of the management plans and the baselines together in one document
        - Quality management plan
        - Scope baseline
    - Project Documents: Any project documents that may need to be updated
        - Project schedule
        - Requirements documentation
        - Risk register
        - Stakeholder register
    - Enterprise Environmental Factors: Factors such as culture, internal systems, and procedures, industry standard
    - Organizational Process Assets: Factors such as processes, procedures and corporate knowledge base
- Tools & Techniques
    - Expert Judgment: Expert technical and/or managerial judgment from and qualified source
    - Data Representation: Techniques such as affinity diagrams and mind mapping to organize ideas in order to generate new ones.
    - Organizational Theory: The body of knowledge that describes how people, teams, and organizations behave
    - Meetings: Used to discuss and address topics that are related to the project. Attendees can include the project team and stakeholders. Meetings can occur in person or virtually
- Outputs
    - Resource Management Plan: The component of the project management plan that provides guidance on how project resources should be categorized, allocated, managed and released

    - Team Charter: A document that establishes the team values, agreements, and operating guidelines for the team
    - Project Documents: Any project documents that may need to be updated
        - Assumption log
        - Risk register

ESTIMATE ACTIVITY RESOURCES

- Definition: The process of estimating team resources and the type and quantities of materials, equipment, and supplies necessary to perform project work
- Inputs
    - Project Management Plan: All of the management plans and the baselines together in one document
        - Resource management plan
        - Scope baseline
    - Project Documents: Any project documents that may need to be updated
        - Activity attributes
        - Activity list
        - Assumption log
        - Cost estimates
        - Resource calendars
        - Risk register
    - Enterprise Environmental Factors: Factors such as culture, internal systems, and procedures, industry standard
    - Organizational Process Assets: Factors such as processes, procedures and corporate knowledge base
- Tools & Techniques
    - Expert Judgment: Expert technical and/or managerial judgment from and qualified source
    - Bottom-Up Estimate: Create an estimate by preparing the lower, detailed work then aggregating into the total quantity of the activity
    - Analogous Estimating: Using previous projects to base current estimates

    - Parametric Estimating: Uses an algorithm or a statistical relationship between historical data and other variables to calculate resource quantities needed for an activity, based on historical data and project parameter
    - Data Analysis: Using techniques such as alternative analysis, cost-benefit analysis, trend analysis and variance analysis to make decisions on the project
    - Project Management Information Systems (PMIS): Includes scheduling software that has the capability to help plan, organize projects
    - Meetings: Used to discuss and address topics that are related to the project. Attendees can include the project team and stakeholders. Meetings can occur in person or virtually
- Outputs
    - Resource Requirements: Identifying the types and quantities of resources required for each work package or activity in a project and can be aggregated to determine the estimated resources for individual work packages, WBS branch and the project as a whole
    - Basis of Estimates: A Document that shows the costs estimates by providing information on how the estimates were calculated such as assumptions, constraints, level of detail, ranges, and confidence levels
    - Resource Breakdown Structure: Identified resources (by category and type)
    - Project Documents Updates: Any updates that are made to the above documents
        - Activity attributes
        - Assumption log
        - Lessons learned register

Acquire Resources

- Definition: Obtaining team members, facilities, equipment, materials, supplies, and other resources necessary to complete project work
- Inputs
    - Project Management Plan: All of the management plans and the baselines together in one document
        - Resource Management Plan
        - Procurement Management Plan
        - Cost Baseline
    - Project Documents: Any project documents that may need to be updated
        - Project schedule

        - Resource calendars
        - Resource requirements
        - Stakeholder register
    - Enterprise Environmental Factors: Factors such as culture, internal systems, and procedures, industry standard
    - Organizational Process Assets: Factors such as processes, procedures and corporate knowledge base
- Tools & Techniques
    - Decision Making: The action or process of making decisions, especially important ones
    - Interpersonal and Team Skills: Soft skills such as personality traits, social graces, communication, language, personal habits, friendliness, and optimism that is important to team development
    - Pre-Assignment: Staff that is already assigned to the project before the acquisition process
    - Virtual Teams: Teams working on the same project but do not necessarily work in the same space
- Outputs
    - Physical resources: Documentation of the physical resource assignments records the material, equipment, supplies, locations and other physical resources that will be used during the project
    - Project Team Assignments: The appropriate people, reliability assigned to staff the project
    - Resource Calendars: Information on the availability of resources over the planned activity duration
    - Change Requests: Requests for changes to scope, schedule, costs, processes or other project documentation
    - Project Management Plan Updates: Any updates to the Project Management Plan as a result of this process
        - Resource management plan
        - Cost baseline
    - Project Documents Updates: Any updates that are made to the above documents
        - Lessons learned register
        - Project schedule
        - Resource breakdown structure

        - Resource requirements
        - Risk register
        - Stakeholder register
    - Enterprise Environmental Factors: Factors such as culture, internal systems, and procedures, industry standard
    - Organizational Process Assets Updates: Updates to Updates to documents such as guidelines, procedures, historical information that is related to the organization

Develop Team

- Definition: Improving competencies, team member interaction, and the overall team environment to enhance project performance
- Input
    - Project Management Plan: All of the management plans and the baselines together in one document
        - Resource management plan
    - Project Documents: Any project documents that may need to be updated
        - Lessons learned register
        - Project schedule
        - Project team assignments
        - Resource calendars
        - Team charter
    - Enterprise Environmental Factors: Factors such as culture, internal systems, and procedures, industry standard
    - Organizational Process Assets: Factors such as processes, procedures and corporate knowledge base
- Tools & Techniques
    - Co-Location: Designating a centralized physical location to enhance team performance
    - Virtual Teams: Teams working on the same project but do not necessarily work in the same space
    - Communication Technology: The practices used to transfer information among project stakeholders (e.g. e-mail, fax, mail, etc.)
    - Interpersonal and Team Skills: Soft skills such as personality traits, social graces, communication, language, personal habits, friendliness, and optimism that is important to team development

- Recognition and Rewards: A technique used by management to reward members of the team when they have performed well
- Training: Activities designed to improve the capabilities of project team members
- Individual and Team Assessments: Tool to help project managers assess team members' preferences, aspirations, how they process and organize information, how they make decisions, and how they interact with people
- Meeting: Discussions with the stakeholders on the progress of the project. Risk management is usually an agenda item

- Outputs
    - Team Performance Assessment: Formal and/or informal assessments of the team's effectiveness
    - Change Requests: Requests for changes to scope, schedule, costs, processes or other project documentation
    - Project Management Plan Updates: Any updates to the Project Management Plan as a result of this process
        - Resource management plan
    - Project Documents Updates: Any updates that are made to the above documents
        - Lessons learned register
        - Project schedule
        - Project team assignments
        - Resource calendars
        - Team charter
    - Enterprise Environmental Factors: Factors such as culture, internal systems, and procedures, industry standard
    - Organizational Process Assets Updates: Updates to Updates to documents such as guidelines, procedures, historical information that is related to the organization

MANAGE TEAM

- Definition: Tracks team member performance by providing feedback, resolving issues and managing team changes to optimize project performance
- Input
    - Project Management Plan: All of the management plans and the baselines together in one document
        - Resource management plan

- Project Documents: Any project documents that may need to be updated
    - Issues log
    - Lessons learned register
    - Project team assignments
    - Team charter
- Work Performance Reports: Reports that summarizes team members performances such as S-curves, bar charts, tables and histograms
- Team Performance Assessment: Formal and/or informal assessments of the team's effectiveness
- Enterprise Environmental Factors: Factors such as culture, internal systems, and procedures, industry standard
- Organizational Process Assets: Factors such as processes, procedures and corporate knowledge base

- Tools & Techniques
    - Interpersonal and Team Skills: Soft skills such as personality traits, social graces, communication, language, personal habits, friendliness, and optimism that is important to team development
    - Project Management Information Systems (PMIS): Includes scheduling software that has the capability to help plan, organize projects
- Outputs
    - Change Requests: Requests for changes to scope, schedule, costs, processes or other project documentation.
    - Project Management Plan Updates: Any updates to the Project Management Plan as a result of this process
        - Resource management plan
        - Schedule baseline
        - Cost baseline
    - Project Documents Updates: Any updates that are made to the above documents
        - Issue log
        - Lessons learned register
        - Project team assignments
    - Enterprise Environmental Factors Updates: Factors such as culture, internal systems, procedures and industry standards updated based on project processes changes

Control Resource

- Definition: Ensuring that the physical resources assigned and allocated to the project are available as planned, as well as monitoring the planned versus actual utilization of resources and taking corrective action as necessary
- Input
  - Project Management Plan: All of the management plans and the baselines together in one document
    - Resource Management Plan
  - Project Documents: Any project documents that may need to be updated
    - Issue log
    - Lessons learned register
    - Physical resource assignment
    - Project schedule
    - Resource breakdown structure
    - Resource Requirements
    - Risk register
  - Work Performance Data: The data that relates to the status, schedule progress, and costs incurred
  - Agreements: Any document or communication that defines the initial intentions of a project. This can take the form of a contract, memo, verbal agreements, email, etc.
  - Organizational Process Assets: Factors such as processes, procedures and corporate knowledge base
- Tools & Techniques
  - Data Analysis: Using techniques such as alternative analysis, cost-benefit analysis, trend analysis and variance analysis to make decisions on the project
  - Problem Solving: Entails finding solutions for issues or challenges. It can include gathering additional information, critical thinking, creative, quantitative and/or logical approaches
  - Interpersonal and Team Skills: Soft skills such as personality traits, social graces, communication, language, personal habits, friendliness, and optimism that is important to team development
  - Project Management Information Systems (PMIS): Includes scheduling software that has the capability to help plan, organize projects

- Outputs
    - Work Performance Information: The actual raw data use used to deliver status, schedule, and cost of the project
    - Change Requests: Requests for changes to scope, schedule, costs, processes or other project documentation
    - Project Management Plan Updates: Any updates to the Project Management Plan as a result of this process
        - Resource management plan
        - Schedule baseline
        - Cost baseline
    - Project Documents Updates: Any updates that are made to the above documents
        - Assumption log
        - Issue log
        - Lessons learned register
        - Physical resource assignments
        - Resource breakdown structure
        - Risk register

Project Communications Management Details

Plan Communications Management

- Definition: Developing an appropriate approach and plan for project communications activities based on the information needs of each stakeholder or group
- Inputs
    - Project Charter: A document that authorizes the project and assigns/authorizes the project manager
    - Project Management Plan: All of the management plans and the baselines together in one document
        - Resource Management Plan
        - Stakeholder engagement plan
    - Project Documents: Any project documents that may need to be updated
        - Requirements documentation
        - Stakeholder register
    - Enterprise Environmental Factors: Factors such as culture, internal systems, and procedures, industry standards
    - Organizational Process Assets: Factors such as processes, procedures and corporate knowledge base
- Tools & Techniques
    - Expert Judgment: Expert technical and/or managerial judgment from and qualified sources
    - Communication Requirements Analysis: The amount information needs among project stakeholders (different stakeholders need different type of information)
    - Communication Technology: The practices used to transfer information among project stakeholders (e.g. e-mail, fax, mail, etc.)
    - Communication Models: A model demonstrating how communication occurs between two parties (e.g. a SOW should always be faxed to the client)
    - Communication Methods: Individual/group meetings, video/audio conferences, and other communication methods
    - Interpersonal and Team Skills: Soft skills such as personality traits, social graces, communication, language, personal habits, friendliness, and optimism that is important to team development

- Data Representation: Techniques such as affinity diagrams and mind mapping to organize ideas in order to generate new ones.
- Meetings: Used to discuss and address topics that are related to the project. Attendees can include the project team and stakeholders. Meetings can occur in person or virtually

- Outputs
  - Communication Management Plan: Details the management of all project communications
  - Project Management Plan Updates: Any updates to the Project Management Plan as a result of this process
    - Stakeholder engagement plan
  - Project Documents Updates: Any updates that are made to the above documents
    - Project schedule
    - Stakeholder register
- Other notes- formula needed:
  - This is where you will use the formula to calculate the number of communication channels on a project: n x (n-12) ÷ 2
  - N=the number of team members/stakeholders on a project

Manage Communications

- Definition: Ensuring timely and appropriate collection, creation, distribution, storage, retrieval, management, monitoring and the ultimate disposition of project information
- Inputs
  - Project Management Plan: All of the management plans and the baselines together in one document
    - Resource management plan
    - Communications management plan
    - Stakeholder engagement plan
  - Project Documents: Any project documents that may need to be updated
    - Change log
    - Issue log
    - Lessons learned register
    - Quality report
    - Risk report

        - Stakeholder register
    - Work Performance Reports: Actual documentation the represents the work performance information compiled in project documents
    - Enterprise Environmental Factors: Factors such as culture, internal systems, and procedures, industry standards
    - Organizational Process Assets: Factors such as processes, procedures and corporate knowledge base
- Tools & Techniques
    - Communication Technology: The practices used to transfer information among project stakeholders (e.g. e-mail, fax, mail, etc.)
    - Communication Methods: Individual/group meetings, video/audio conferences, and other communication methods
    - Communication Skills: Techniques such as feedback, presentation, non-verbal (e.g. body language)
    - Project Management Information Systems (PMIS): Includes scheduling software that has the capability to help plan, organize projects
    - Project Reporting: The act of collecting and distributing project information
    - Interpersonal and Team Skills: Soft skills such as personality traits, social graces, communication, language, personal habits, friendliness, and optimism that is important to team development
    - Meeting: Discussions with the stakeholders on the progress of the project. Risk management is usually an agenda item
- Outputs
    - Project Communications: How activities are created, distributed, received, acknowledged and understood. Such as status reports, schedule progress, etc.
    - Project Management Plan Updates: Any updates to the Project Management Plan as a result of this process
        - Communications management plan
        - Stakeholder engagement plan
    - Project Documents Updates: Any updates that are made to the above documents
        - Issues log
        - Lessons learned register
        - Project schedule
        - Risk register

        - Stakeholder register
    - Organizational Process Assets Updates: Updates to documents such as guidelines, procedures, historical information that is related to the organization

MONITOR COMMUNICATIONS

- Definition: Ensuring the information needs of the project and its stakeholders are met
- Inputs
    - Project Management Plan: all of the management plans and the baselines together in one document
        - Resource management plan
        - Communications plan
        - Stakeholder engagement
    - Project Documents: Any project documents that may need to be updated
        - Issue log
        - Lessons learned register
        - Project Communications
    - Work Performance Data: The data that relates to the status, schedule progress, and costs incurred
    - Enterprise Environmental Factors: Factors such as culture, internal systems and procedures, industry standard
    - Organizational Process Assets: Factors such as processes, procedures and corporate knowledge base
- Tools & Techniques
    - Expert Judgment: Expert technical and/or managerial judgment from and qualified sources
    - Project Management Information Systems (PMIS): Includes scheduling software that has the capability to help plan, organize projects
    - Data Analysis: Using techniques such as alternative analysis, cost-benefit analysis, trend analysis and variance analysis to make decisions on the project
        - Stakeholder engagement assessment matrix
    - Interpersonal and Team Skills: Soft skills such as personality traits, social graces, communication, language, personal habits, friendliness, and optimism that is important to team development

    - Meetings: Used to discuss and address topics that are related to the project. Attendees can include the project team and stakeholders. Meetings can occur in person or virtually
- Outputs
    - Work Performance Information: The actual raw data use used to deliver status, schedule, and cost of the project
    - Change Requests: Requests for changes to scope, schedule, costs, processes or other project documentation.
    - Project Management Plan Updates: Any updates to the Project Management Plan as a result of this process
        - Communications management plan
        - Stakeholder engagement plan
    - Project Documents Updates: Any updates that are made to the above documents
        - Issue log
        - Lessons learned register
        - Stakeholder register

- Other notes- about meetings:
    - Give out agenda ahead of time
    - Needs to be time stamp
    - Must do an attendees analysis
    - Distribute meeting notes at end of meeting

Project Risk Management Details

Plan Risk Management

- Definition: Defines how risk management will be accomplished for a project
- Inputs
    - Project Charter: A document that authorizes the project and assigns/authorizes the project manager
    - Project Management Plan: All of the management plans and the baselines together in one document
        - All components
    - Enterprise Environmental Factors: Factors such as culture, internal systems, and procedures, industry standard
    - Organizational Process Assets: Factors such as processes, procedures and corporate knowledge base
- Tools & Techniques
    - Expert Judgment: Expert technical and/or managerial judgment from and qualified sources
    - Data Analysis: Using techniques such as alternative analysis, cost-benefit analysis, trend analysis and variance analysis to make decisions on the project
        - Stakeholder analysis
    - Meetings: Used to discuss and address topics that are related to the project. Attendees can include the project team and stakeholders. Meetings can occur in person or virtually
- Outputs
    - Risk Management Plan: The actual plan that details project risk, how to manage it and the way it will be structured within the project

Identify Risks

- Definition: Determines potential project risks and documents their characteristics
- Inputs
    - Project Management Plan: All of the management plans and the baselines together in one document
        - Requirements management plan

        - Schedule management plan
        - Cost management plan
        - Quality management plan
        - Resource management plan
        - Risk management plan
        - Scope baseline
        - Schedule baseline
        - Cost baseline
    - Project Documents: Additional project documentation that aids in identification of risks
        - Assumption log
        - Cost estimates
        - Duration estimates
        - Issue log
        - Lessons learned register
        - Requirements documentation
        - Resource requirements
        - Stakeholder register
    - Agreements: Any document or communication that defines the initial intentions of a project. This can take the form of a contract, memo, verbal agreements, email, etc.
    - Procurement Documentation: Used to demonstrate compliance with the project scope
    - Enterprise Environmental Factors: Factors such as culture, internal systems, and procedures, industry standard
    - Organizational Process Assets: Factors such as processes, procedures and corporate knowledge base
- Tools & Techniques
    - Expert Judgment: Expert technical and/or managerial judgment from and qualified sources
    - Data Gathering: Techniques such as brainstorming, focus groups and interviews to gather information
    - Data Analysis: Using techniques such as alternative analysis, cost-benefit analysis, trend analysis and variance analysis to make decisions on the project

    - Interpersonal and Team Skills: Soft skills such as personality traits, social graces, communication, language, personal habits, friendliness, and optimism that is important to team development
    - Prompt Lists: A predetermined list of risk categories that might give rise to individual project risks and that could also act as sources of overall project risk
    - Meeting: Discussions with the stakeholders on the progress of the project. Risk management is usually an agenda item
- Outputs
    - Risk Register: List of identified risks
    - Risk Report: Presents information on sources of overall project risk, together with summary information on identified individual project risks
    - Project Documents Updates: Any updates that are made to the above documents
        - Assumption log
        - Issue log
        - Lessons learned register

Perform Qualitative Risk Analysis

- Definition: Prioritizes risks by analyzing their combined probability and impact
- Inputs
    - Project Management Plan: All of the management plans and the baselines together in one document
        - Risk management plan
    - Project Documents: Any project documents that may need to be updated
        - Assumption log
        - Risk register
        - Stakeholder register
    - Enterprise Environmental Factors: Factors such as culture, internal systems, and procedures, industry standard
    - Organizational Process Assets: Factors such as processes, procedures and corporate knowledge base
- Tools & Techniques
    - Expert Judgment: Expert technical and/or managerial judgment from and qualified sources

    - Data Gathering: Techniques such as brainstorming, focus groups and interviews to gather information
    - Data Analysis: Using techniques such as alternative analysis, cost-benefit analysis, trend analysis and variance analysis to make decisions on the project
    - Interpersonal and Team Skills: Soft skills such as personality traits, social graces, communication, language, personal habits, friendliness, and optimism that is important to team development
    - Risk Categorization: The different types of risks: Technical, external, project management and organizational
    - Data Representation: Techniques such as affinity diagrams and mind mapping to organize ideas in order to generate new ones
    - Meeting: Discussions with the stakeholders on the progress of the project. Risk management is usually an agenda item
- Outputs
    - Project Documents Updates: Any updates that are made to the above documents
        - Assumption log
        - Issue log
        - Risk register
        - Risk report

PERFORM QUANTITATIVE RISK ANALYSIS

- Define: Numerically analyze the effect of risk on overall project objectives that focus on the overall cost of the project
- Inputs
    - Project Management Plan: All of the management plans and the baselines together in one document
        - Risk Management Plan
        - Scope baseline
        - Schedule baseline
        - Cost baseline
    - Project Documents: Any project documents that may need to be updated
        - Assumption log
        - Basis of estimates

        - Cost estimates
        - Cost forecasts
        - Duration of estimators
        - Milestone list
        - Resource requirements
        - Risk register
        - Risk report
        - Schedule forecasts
    - Enterprise Environmental Factors: Factors such as culture, internal systems, and procedures, industry standard
    - Organizational Process Assets: Factors such as processes, procedures and corporate knowledge base
- Tools & Techniques
    - Expert Judgment: Expert technical and/or managerial judgment from and qualified sources
    - Data Gathering: Techniques such as brainstorming, focus groups and interviews to gather information
    - Interpersonal and Team Skills: Soft skills such as personality traits, social graces, communication, language, personal habits, friendliness, and optimism that is important to team development
    - Representations of Uncertainty: Inputs to a quantitative risk analysis model that reflect individual project risks and other sources of uncertainty. For example, where the duration, cost, or resource requirements for a planned activity is uncertain, the range of possible values can be represented in the model as a probability distribution
    - Data Analysis: Using techniques such as alternative analysis, cost-benefit analysis, trend analysis and variance analysis to make decisions on the project
- Outputs
    - Project Documents Updates: Any updates that make the above documents
        - Risk report

Plan Risk Responses

- Define: Develops options & actions to reduce threats and enhance opportunities
- Inputs

- Project Management Plan: All of the management plans and the baselines together in one document
    - Resource management plan
    - Risk management plan
    - Cost baseline
- Project Documents: Any project documents that may need to be updated
    - Lessons learned register
    - Project schedule
    - Project team assignments
    - Resource calendars
    - Risk register
    - Risk report
    - Stakeholder register
- Enterprise Environmental Factors: Factors such as culture, internal systems, and procedures, industry standard
- Organizational Process Assets: Factors such as processes, procedures and corporate knowledge base

- Tools & Techniques
    - Expert Judgment: Expert technical and/or managerial judgment from and qualified sources
    - Data Gathering: Techniques such as brainstorming, focus groups and interviews to gather information
    - Interpersonal and Team Skills: Soft skills such as personality traits, social graces, communication, language, personal habits, friendliness, and optimism that is important to team development
    - Strategies for Threats: Five alternative strategies may be considered for dealing with threats: Escalate, avoid, transfer, mitigate, accept
    - Strategies for Opportunities: Five alternative strategies may be considered for dealing with opportunities: Escalate, exploit, share, enhance, accept
    - Contingent Response Strategies: Various response plans that will be used under certain circumstances or events
    - Strategies for Overall Project Risk: Risk responses should be planned for the overall project using one or more of these strategies: avoid, exploit, transfer/share, mitigate/enhance, accept

    - Data Analysis: Using techniques such as alternative analysis, cost-benefit analysis, trend analysis and variance analysis to make decisions on the project
    - Decision Making: The action or process of making decisions, especially important ones
- Outputs
    - Change Requests: Requests for changes to scope, schedule, costs, processes or other project documentation
    - Project Management Plan Updates: Any updates to the Project Management Plan as a result of this process
        - Schedule management plan
        - Cost management plan
        - Quality management plan
        - Resource management plan
        - Procurement management plan
        - Scope baseline
        - Schedule baseline
        - Cost baseline
    - Project Documents Updates: Any updates that are made to the above documents
        - Assumption log
        - Cost forecasts
        - Lessons learned register
        - Project schedule
        - Project team assignments
        - Risk Register
        - Risk report
- Other note-Strategy definitions of the risks threats and opportunities:
    - Acceptance=It is what it is
    - Avoid= Eliminate
    - Mitigate= Reduce
    - Transfer= Shift
    - Escalate= Tell authority
    - Exploit= Add
    - Enhance= Increase

    - Share=Include third party

Implement Risk

- Definition: Executes risk response plans and evaluates their effectiveness
- Inputs
    - Project Management Plan: all of the management plans and the baselines together in one document
        - Risk management plan
    - Project Documents: Any project documents that may need to be updated
        - Lessons learned register
        - Risk register
        - Risk report
    - Organizational Process Assets: Factors such as processes, procedures and corporate knowledge base
- Tools & Techniques
    - Expert Judgment: Expert technical and/or managerial judgment from and qualified sources
    - Interpersonal and Team Skills: Soft skills such as personality traits, social graces, communication, language, personal habits, friendliness, and optimism that is important to team development
    - Project Management Information Systems (PMIS): Includes scheduling software that has the capability to help plan, organize projects
- Outputs
    - Change Requests: Requests for changes to scope, schedule, costs, processes or other project documentation
    - Project Documents Updates: Any updates that are made to the above documents
        - Issue log
        - Lessons learned register
        - Project team assignments
        - Risk register
        - Risk report

MONITOR RISKS

- Definition: Monitoring the implementation of agreed-upon risk response plans, tracking identified risks, identifying and analyzing new risks, and evaluating risk process effectiveness throughout the project
- Inputs
    - Project Management Plan: All of the management plans and the baselines together in one document
        - Risk management plan
    - Project Documents: Any project documents that may need to be updated
        - Issue log
        - Lessons learned register
        - Risk register
        - Risk report
    - Work Performance Data: The data that relates to the status, schedule progress, and costs incurred
    - Work Performance Reports: Reports that summarizes team members performances such as S-curves, bar charts, tables and histograms
- Tools & Techniques
    - Data Analysis: Using techniques such as alternative analysis, cost-benefit analysis, trend analysis and variance analysis to make decisions on the project
    - Audits: Structured, independent process used to determine if project activities comply with organizational and project policies, processes and procedure
    - Meetings: Discussions with the stakeholders on the progress of the project. Risk management is usually an agenda item

Outputs
    - Work Performance Information: The actual raw data use used to deliver status, schedule, and cost of the project
    - Change Requests: Requests for changes to scope, schedule, costs, processes or other project documentation
    - Project Management Plan Updates: Any updates to the Project Management Plan as a result of this process
        - Any component

- Project Documents Updates: Any updates that are made to the above documents
  - Assumption log
  - Issue log
  - Lessons learned register
  - Risk register
  - Risk report
- Organizational Process Assets Updates: Updates to Updates to documents such as guidelines, procedures, historical information that is related to the organization

Project Procurement Management Details

Plan Procurement Management

- Definition: Document purchasing decisions, the procurement approach, and identify potential sellers
- Inputs
  - Project Charter: A document that authorizes the project and assigns/authorizes the project manager
  - Business Documents: Any sources of information about the project's objectives and how the project will contribute to the business goals
    - Business case
    - Benefits management plan
  - Project Management Plan: All of the management plans and the baselines together in one document
    - Scope management plan
    - Quality management plan
    - Resource management plan
    - Scope baseline
  - Project Documents: Any project documents that may need to be updated
    - Milestone list
    - Project team assignments
    - Requirements documentation
    - Requirements traceability matrix
    - Resource requirements
    - Risk register
    - Stakeholder register
  - Enterprise Environmental Factors: Factors such as culture, internal systems, and procedures, industry standard
  - Organizational Process Assets: Factors such as processes, procedures and corporate knowledge base

- Tools & Techniques
    - Expert Judgment: Expert technical and/or managerial judgment from and qualified sources
    - Data Gathering: Techniques such as brainstorming, focus groups and interviews to gather information
    - Data Analysis: Using techniques such as alternative analysis, cost-benefit analysis, trend analysis and variance analysis to make decisions on the project
    - Source Selection Analysis: Measurements that are used to help determine the right proposals submitted by prospective project suppliers
    - Meetings: Discussions with the stakeholders on the progress of the project. Risk management is usually an agenda item
- Outputs
    - Procurement Management Plan: A plan that describes how the procurement process will be managed
    - Procurement Strategy: To determine the project delivery method, the type of legally binding agreement(s), and how the procurement will advance through the procurement phases
    - Bid Documents: All documents used to solicit information, quotations, or proposals from the prospective sellers
    - Procurement Statements of Work: A list and description of each procurement item from prospective sellers
    - Source Selection Criteria: Measurements that are used to help determine the right proposals submitted by prospective project suppliers
    - Make-or-Buy Decisions: The documentation decisions of what will be developed in-house and what will be purchased outside the organization
    - Independent Cost Estimate: Estimates that has been estimated to be used as benchmarks for the submitted proposals from suppliers/sellers
    - Change Requests: Requests for changes to scope, schedule, costs, processes or other project documentation
    - Project Documents Updates: Any updates that are made to the above documents
        - Lessons learned register
        - Milestone list
        - Requirements documentation
        - Requirements traceability matrix
        - Risk register

        - Stakeholder register
    - Organizational Process Assets Updates: Updates to Updates to documents such as guidelines, procedures, historical information that is related to the organization

CONDUCT PROCUREMENTS

- Definition: Obtaining seller responses, selecting sellers and awarding contract
- Inputs
    - Project Management Plan: All of the management plans and the baselines together in one document
        - Scope management plan
        - Requirements management plan
        - Communications management plan
        - Risk management plan
        - Procurement management plan
        - Configuration management plan
        - Cost baseline
    - Project Documents: Additional project documentation that aids in identification of risks
        - Lessons learned register
        - Project schedule
        - Requirements documentation
        - Risk register
        - Stakeholder register
    - Procurement Documentation: Used to demonstrate compliance with the project scope
    - Seller Proposals: Sellers/suppliers that describe the ability and availability to provide requested services
    - Enterprise Environmental Factors: Factors such as culture, internal systems, and procedures, industry standard
    - Organizational Process Assets: Factors such as processes, procedures and corporate knowledge base
- Tools & Techniques
    - Expert Judgment: Expert technical and/or managerial judgment from and qualified sources
    - Advertising: Advertisements used to receive potential sellers for contracted services and/or goods.

- Bidder Conferences: Meetings with the prospective project suppliers/sellers where they can ask questions and receive answers pertaining to the project prior to preparing the proposal
- Data Analysis: Using techniques such as alternative analysis, cost-benefit analysis, trend analysis and variance analysis to make decisions on the project
- Interpersonal and Team Skills: Soft skills such as personality traits, social graces, communication, language, personal habits, friendliness, and optimism that is important to team development

- Outputs
  - Selected Sellers: The final list of sellers/suppliers
  - Agreements: Although it's a document, this will be used as in input if the project is accepted for the external customer and/or client. This can be contracts, memorandums, service level agreements (SLA), letter of intent, verbal agreements, e-mails, etc.
  - Change Requests: Requests for changes to scope, schedule, costs, processes or other project documentation.
  - Project Management Plan Updates: Any updates to the Project Management Plan as a result of this process
    - Requirements management plan
    - Quality management plan
    - Communications management plan
    - Risk management plan
    - Procurement management plan
    - Scope baseline
    - Schedule baseline
    - Cost baseline
  - Project Documents Updates: Any updates that are made to the above documents
    - Lessons learned register
    - Requirements documentation
    - Requirements traceability matrix
    - Risk register
    - Stakeholder register
  - Organizational Process Assets Updates: Updates to Updates to documents such as guidelines, procedures, historical information that is related to the organization

Control Procurements

- Definition: Managing procurement relationships and contract performance
- Inputs
  - Project Management Plan: All of the management plans and the baselines together in one document
    - Requirements management plan
    - Risk management plan
    - Procurement management plan
    - Change management plan
    - Schedule baseline
  - Procurement Documents: Lists procurement contract stakeholders
    - Assumption log
    - Lessons learned register
    - Milestone list
    - Quality reports
    - Requirements documentation
    - Requirements traceability matrix
    - Risk register
    - Stakeholder register
  - Agreements: Although it's a document, this will be used as in input if the project is accepted for the external customer and/or client. This can be contracts, memorandums, service level agreements (SLA), letter of intent, verbal agreements, e-mails, etc.
  - Procurement Documentation: Used to demonstrate compliance with the project scope
  - Approved Change Requests: A documentation that shows all authorized changes that expand or reduce scope
  - Work Performance Data: The data that relates to the status, schedule progress, and costs incurred
  - Enterprise Environmental Factors: Factors such as culture, internal systems, and procedures, industry standard

- Organizational Process Assets: Factors such as processes, procedures and corporate knowledge base

- Tools & Techniques
  - Expert Judgment: Expert technical and/or managerial judgment from and qualified sources
  - Claims Administration: The process and procedures of resolving disputes and contested changes between the buyer and seller
  - Data Analysis: Using techniques such as alternative analysis, cost-benefit analysis, trend analysis and variance analysis to make decisions on the project
  - Inspection: An examination to ensure the end results are to expected requirements. Could be done through an audit, walkthrough or formal review
  - Audits: Structured, independent process used to determine if project activities comply with organizational and project policies, processes and procedure
- Outputs
  - Closed Procurements: A formal notice that the procurements have been closed
  - Work Performance Information: The data that relates to the status, schedule progress, and costs incurred
  - Procurement Documentation Updates: Procurement documentation that may be updated includes the contract with all supporting schedules, requested unapproved contract changes, and approved change request
  - Change Requests: Requests for changes to scope, schedule, costs, processes or other project documentation.
  - Project Management Plan Updates: Any updates to the Project Management Plan as a result of this process
    - Risk management plan
    - Procurement management plan
    - Schedule baseline
    - Cost baseline
  - Project Documents Updates: Any updates that are made to the above documents
    - Lessons learned register
    - Resource requirements
    - Requirements traceability matrix

        - Risk register
        - Stakeholder register
    - Organizational Process Assets Updates: Updates to Updates to documents such as guidelines, procedures, historical information that is related to the organization

PROJECT STAKEHOLDER MANAGEMENT DETAILS

IDENTIFY STAKEHOLDERS

- Definition: Identify the people, groups, and/or organizations that have an impact on the project
- Inputs
    - Project Charter: A document that authorizes the project and assigns/authorizes the project manager
    - Business Documents: Any sources of information about the project's objectives and how the project will contribute to the business goals
        - Business case
        - Benefits management plan
    - Project Management Plan: All of the management plans and the baselines together in one document
        - Communications management plan
        - Stakeholder engagement plan
    - Project Documents: Any project documents that may need to be updated
        - Change log
        - Issue log
        - Requirements documentation
    - Agreements: Any document or communication that defines the initial intentions of a project. This can take the form of a contract, memo, verbal agreements, email, etc.
    - Enterprise Environmental Factors: Factors such as culture, internal systems, and procedures, industry standard
    - Organizational Process Assets: Factors such as processes, procedures and corporate knowledge base
- Tools & Techniques
    - Expert Judgment: Expert technical and/or managerial judgment from and qualified sources

- Data Gathering: Techniques such as brainstorming, focus groups and interviews to gather information
- Data Analysis: Using techniques such as alternative analysis, cost-benefit analysis, trend analysis and variance analysis to make decisions on the project
- Data Representation: Techniques such as affinity diagrams and mind mapping to organize ideas in order to generate new ones.
- Meetings: Discussions with the stakeholders on the progress of the project. Risk management is usually an agenda item

- Outputs
    - Stakeholder Register: A document that lists all project stakeholder information
    - Change Requests: Requests for changes to scope, schedule, costs, processes or other project documentation
    - Project Management Plan: All of the management plans and the baselines together in one document
        - Requirements management plan
        - Communications management plan
        - Risk management plan
        - Stakeholder engagement plan
    - Project Documents Updates: Any updates that are made to the above documents
        - Assumption log
        - Issue log
        - Risk register

Plan Stakeholders Management

- Definition: Developing appropriate strategy to manage and engage stakeholders throughout the project lifecycle
- Inputs
    - Project Charter: A document that authorizes the project and assigns/authorizes the project manager
    - Project Management Plan: All of the management plans and the baselines together in one document
        - Resource management plan
        - Communications management plan

        - Risk management plan
    - Project Documents: Any project documents that may need to be updated
        - Assumption log
        - Change log
        - Issue log
        - Project schedule
        - Risk register
        - Stakeholder register
    - Agreements: Any document or communication that defines the initial intentions of a project. This can take the form of a contract, memo, verbal agreements, email, etc.
    - Enterprise Environmental Factors: Factors such as culture, internal systems, and procedures, industry standard
    - Organizational Process Assets: Factors such as processes, procedures and corporate knowledge base
- Tools & Techniques
    - Expert Judgment: Expert technical and/or managerial judgment from and qualified sources
    - Data Gathering: Techniques such as brainstorming, focus groups and interviews to gather information
    - Data Analysis: Using techniques such as alternative analysis, cost-benefit analysis, trend analysis and variance analysis to make decisions on the project
    - Decision Making: The action or process of making decisions, especially important ones
    - Data Representation: Techniques such as affinity diagrams and mind mapping to organize ideas in order to generate new ones.
    - Meetings: Discussions with the stakeholders on the progress of the project. Risk management is usually an agenda item
- Outputs
    - Stakeholder Engagement Plan: A document that lists all project stakeholder information and how to manage

MANAGE STAKEHOLDERS ENGAGEMENT

- Definition: Manage communications to satisfy stakeholder requirements
- Inputs

- Project Management Plan: All of the management plans and the baselines together in one document
    - Communications management plan
    - Risk management plan
    - Stakeholder engagement plan
- Project Documents: Any project documents that may need to be updated
    - Change log
    - Issue log
    - Lessons learned register
    - Stakeholder register
- Enterprise Environmental Factors: Factors such as culture, internal systems, and procedures, industry standard
- Organizational Process Assets: Factors such as processes, procedures and corporate knowledge base

- Tools & Techniques
    - Expert Judgment: Expert technical and/or managerial judgment from and qualified sources
    - Communication Skills: Techniques such as feedback, presentation, non-verbal (e.g. body language)
    - Interpersonal and Team Skills: Soft skills such as personality traits, social graces, communication, language, personal habits, friendliness, and optimism that is important to team development
    - Ground Rules: A Document that lists out team rules to set expectations with all of the team members on acceptable behavior
    - Meeting: Discussions with the stakeholders on the progress of the project. Risk management is usually an agenda item
- Outputs
    - Change Requests: Requests for changes to scope, schedule, costs, processes or other project documentation
    - Project Management Plan Updates: Any updates to the Project Management Plan as a result of this process
        - Communications management plan
        - Stakeholder engagement plan
    - Project Documents Updates: Any updates that are made to the above documents

        - Change log
        - Issue log
        - Lessons learned register
        - Stakeholder register

Monitor Stakeholders Engagement

- Definition: Manage communications to satisfy stakeholder requirements
- Inputs
    - Project Management Plan: all of the management plans and the baselines together in one document
        - Resource management plan
        - Communications management plan
        - Stakeholder engagement plan
    - Project Documents: Additional project documentation that aids in identification of risks
        - Issue log
        - Lessons learned register
        - Project communications
        - Risk register
        - Stakeholder register
    - Work Performance Data: The data that relates to the status, schedule progress, and costs incurred
    - Enterprise Environmental Factors: Factors such as culture, internal systems, and procedures, industry standard
    - Organizational Process Assets: Factors such as processes, procedures and corporate knowledge base
- Tools & Techniques
    - Data Analysis: Using techniques such as alternative analysis, cost-benefit analysis, trend analysis and variance analysis to make decisions on the project
    - Decision Making: The action or process of making decisions, especially important ones
    - Data Representation: Techniques such as affinity diagrams and mind mapping to organize ideas in order to generate new ones.
    - Communication Skills: Techniques such as feedback, presentation, non-verbal (e.g. body language)

- Interpersonal and Team Skills: Soft skills such as personality traits, social graces, communication, language, personal habits, friendliness, and optimism that is important to team development
- Meetings: Discussions with the stakeholders on the progress of the project. Risk management is usually an agenda item

- Outputs
  - Work Performance Information: The data that relates to the status, schedule progress, and costs incurred
  - Change Requests: Requests for changes to scope, schedule, costs, processes or other project documentation.
  - Project Management Plan Updates: Any updates to the Project Management Plan as a result of this process
    - Resource management plan
    - Communications management plan
    - Stakeholder engagement plan
  - Project Documents Updates: Any updates that are made to the above documents
    - Issue log
    - Lessons learned register
    - Risk register
    - Stakeholder register

FORMULAS

BAC=Budget At Completion

PV= (Planned%) BAC

EV= Actual % complete x BAC

AC= Total Money Spent

CV=EV-AC

SV= EV-PV

CPI= EV ÷ AC

$CPI^c = EV^c \div AC^c$

SPI= EV ÷ PV

$EAC = BAC \div CPI^c$

ETC= EAC – AC

VAC= BAC-EAC

$TCPI_c$ = (BAC-EV)/Remaining Funds

Channels=n(n-1)/2

What each equation means:

- BAC=Budget At Completion
    - How much money will be spent on the project
- PV= Planned Value
    - Determines how much should have been spent based on the schedule
- EV= Earned Value
    - How much of the project's value that was truly earned
- AC= Actual Cost
    - How much has been spent at any particular point during the project
- CV= Cost Variance
    - Calculates if the project is over or under budget
- SV= Schedule Variance
    - Calculates if the project is ahead or behind schedule monetarily
    - Why: Give a monetary value of the schedule

- CPI= Cost Performance Index
    - Determines if the project is within budget
    - If the CPI is below 1, then the project is over budget
    - If the CPI is much bigger than 1, the project is under budget
- SPI= Schedule Performance Index
    - Calculates if the project is ahead or behind schedule
    - If the SPI is below 1, then the project is behind schedule
- TCPI= To complete Performance Index
    - Calculates how well the project must perform to stay on budget
    - Higher number means that the project is running hot in terms of the budget
- EAC= Estimate At Completion
    - Prediction on when the total cost of the project when completed
- ETC= Estimate To Completion
    - Determines how much more money needed to spend on the project
- VAC= Variance At Completion
    - Estimates what the variance of the cost will be when the project is done

List of Project Management Plan and Project Documents

Project Management Plan

- Scope management plan
- Requirements management plan
- Schedule management plan
- Cost management plan
- Quality management plan
- Resource management plan
- Communications management plan
- Risk management plan
- Procurement management plan
- Stakeholder engagement plan
- Change management plan
- Configuration management plan
- Scope baseline
- Schedule baseline
- Cost baseline
- Performance measurement baseline
- Project life cycle description
- Development approach

Project Documents

- Activity attributes
- Activity list
- Assumption log
- Basis of estimates
- Change log
- Cost estimates
- Cost forecasts

- Duration estimates
- Cost forecasts
- Duration estimates
- Issue log
- Lessons learned register
- Milestone list
- Physical resource assignments
- Project calendars
- Project communications
- Project schedule
- Project schedule network diagram
- Project scope statement
- Project team assignments
- Quality control measurements
- Quality metrics
- Quality report
- Requirements documentation
- Requirements traceability matrix
- Resource breakdown structure
- Resource calendars
- Resource requirements
- Risk register
- Risk report
- Schedule data
- Schedule forecasts
- Stakeholder register
- Team charter
- Test and evaluation documents

PROJECT MANAGEMENT ETHICS

1. Follow all laws and company policies
2. Treat everyone with respect and fairly
3. Respect the community and the environment
4. Give back to the project management community
5. Keep learning and growing as a project manager
6. Respect other people's' culture
7. Respect copyright laws
8. Be honest with everyone on the project
9. If someone lied, about being PMP certified, stolen PMP questions or cheated on the exam, you must report them to PMI

Fun and Interesting PM Resources

Head PM in Charge (https://www.cafepress.com/pmincharge)

Whether you passed your exam, all project managers are PiMPs: Professional Intellects that Manage Projects. You can find fun ways of showing off your PiMP status and tell them who is in charge

ThePMPNotebook.com

Stay in touch and get the latest news on the PMP Notebook such as updated versions or information about the exam.

About the Author

Kaye I. Smith-Bedeau is a certified integrated project manager with experience implementing campaigns designed to maximize brand and product exposure on multiple platforms. She's helped agencies and organizations improve their project operation systems including overall client operations, CRM, marketing and content development. Her experience includes offline, online and digital space including social media integration. Some of her industry experience includes retail, television, publication, music, food/beverages, technology, nonprofit and financial institutions.

Kaye has also taught communications and marketing classes at a leading virtual university to share her experience with other students who are embarking on new professional endeavors.

Kaye holds a MBA, Masters in Project Management and earned the Project Management Certification (PMP) from the Project Management Institute (PMI).

You can contact Kaye at Kayesmithpmp@gmail.com